Smart Animals

PARROTS

by Margaret Fetty

Consultant: Karl Kranz
General Curator
The Maryland Zoo in Baltimore

BEARPORT
PUBLISHING COMPANY, INC.

New York, New York

Credits

Cover (center), Colleen Coombe/istockphoto; Cover (background), Kevin Tate/istockphoto; Title Page, Collen Coombe/istockphoto; 4, Time & Life Pictures/Getty Images; 5, Alex Foundation; 6, Frank Siteman/Index Stock Photo; 7, Aimee Morgana; 8, Aimee Morgana; 9, Roy Berger; 10, William D. Bachman/Photo Researchers, Inc.; 11, Sally Blanchard; 12, Bill Beatty/Animals Animals/Earth Scenes; 13, Kathleen Carr/Indiana University; 14, Craig K. Lorenz/Photo Researchers, Inc.; 15, Mark Newman/Index Stock; 16, Myrleen Cate/Index Stock; 17, Royalty-Free/Corbis; 18, Roy Berger; 19, Royalty-Free/Photodisc Blue/Getty Images; 20, Ian Murphy/Getty Images; 20 (map), Dave Herring; 21(t), Lynn Stone; 21(b), William D. Bachman/Photo Researchers, Inc.; 22, Mark I. Stafford/Parrot International; 23, Mark I. Stafford/Parrot International; 24, Art Wolfe/Photo Researchers, Inc; 25, Mitsuaki Iwago/Minden Pictures; 26, Kenneth W. Fink/Photo Researchers, Inc.; 27, David Grossman/Photo Researchers, Inc.; 28(l), Lynn Stone; 28(r), Jack Hollingsworth/Asia Images/Getty Images; 29, Carlos Adolfo Sastoque N./SuperStock.

Design and production by Dawn Beard Creative and Octavo Design and Production, Inc.

Library of Congress Cataloging-in-Publication Data

Fetty, Margaret.
  Parrots / by Margaret Fetty.
      p. cm.—(Smart animals!)
  Includes bibliographical references and index.
  ISBN-13: 978-1-59716-163-3 (library binding)
  ISBN-10: 1-59716-163-2 (library binding)
  ISBN-13: 978-1-59716-189-3 (pbk.)
  ISBN-10: 1-59716-189-6 (pbk.)
  1. Parrots—Psychology—Juvenile literature. 2. Animal communication—Juvenile literature. 3. Learning in animals—Juvenile literature. I. Title. II. Series.

  QL696.P7F48 2006
  598.7'1—dc22

                            2005028038

For more information, write to Bearport Publishing Company, Inc., 101 Fifth Avenue, Suite 6R, New York, New York 10003. Printed in the United States of America.

10 9 8 7 6 5 4 3 2

Contents

Look Who's Talking!

Dr. Irene Pepperberg shows Alex a group of objects. They are different colors and shapes. They are made out of different **materials**. Dr. Pepperberg asks Alex to find the orange object with three corners and tell what kind of material it is made out of. Alex looks carefully at the shapes. Finally, Alex answers "wool." Alex is right!

◄ **Alex looks at each object before he picks the right one.**

Some scientists believe that African gray parrots can solve problems as well as a child who is four years old.

It may seem easy to pick out an object and name its material. Yet scientists are quite excited about Alex's skill. Why? Alex is an African gray parrot! He can talk. He can identify colors, shapes, and materials. Alex can even **communicate** with people.

▲ Alex is learning the sounds that different letters make.

Language Learners

Parrots are one of the few animals that can say words in a human **language**. Just like small children, parrots learn to speak words by listening to people talk. Scientists believe that using language is a sign of a smart animal.

▲ The yellow-naped Amazon parrot, like the African gray, is very good at saying human words.

Alex is not the only parrot who can talk. N'kisi (in-KEE-see) is another African gray parrot. He knows over 1,100 words! N'kisi can even put words in the correct order to make sentences.

When N'kisi speaks, he can use words to show he knows the difference between past, present, and future.

▲ **N'kisi**

Making New Words

N'kisi doesn't just use words in sentences. N'kisi takes words he knows and puts them together to describe something that is new to him.

One time, N'kisi's owner had some bath oil. It smelled sweet. N'kisi had never seen or smelled bath oil before. He called the oil "pretty smell medicine."

◀ **N'kisi learns words and sounds using letter cards.**

Some scientists say that joining words to name something new shows that an animal is **intelligent**. This skill shows that the animal is thinking.

▲ African gray parrots that have been raised by people may begin to make human sounds just a few weeks after they hatch.

Like parrots, chimps have put words together to name things they have never seen before. However, chimps use sign language to communicate instead of spoken words.

Understanding Language

Some people say that parrots only **mimic**, or repeat, the words they hear. They believe the birds do not understand what they are saying. Sally Blanchard, however, believes that parrots really do understand language.

▲ Budgerigars (BUH-juh-ree-*garz*) are small parrots that are also called parakeets. Many male parakeets are excellent talkers. In 1958, Sparkie the parakeet made it into the *Guinness Book of World Records* for saying eight nursery rhymes in one breath.

Sally taught her parrot Bongo Marie how to make animal sounds. In all, the bird learned 12 different animal noises. One day, Sally called out to Bongo Marie, "Hey, turkey!" Bongo Marie replied, "Gobble, gobble, gobble."

Another time Bongo Marie was ripping apart a cereal box. Sally asked, "What are you doing?" Bongo Marie answered, "None of your business."

Parrots can say most letters of the alphabet. However, they cannot clearly say words that have *l* or *r* sounds.

◀ **Sally Blanchard and Bongo Marie**

Tongues That Talk

Scientists wondered why parrots are one of the few birds that can make human sounds. They compared the tongues of parrots to other birds.

Most birds have skinny, pointed tongues. Many of them eat nuts with thin shells. So they can use just their **beaks** to open the nuts.

▲ Red-bellied woodpeckers eat nuts, fruit, and insects. Like many other birds, they have thin, skinny tongues.

Parrots, however, eat nuts that have hard shells. So they have differently shaped tongues. The tongues are thick and round to help their sharp beaks break open the hard nuts. These tongues move easily, which help the parrots make sounds like humans.

▲ **The thick, round tongues of parrots help them speak.**

In addition to tongues, parrots use their syrinx (SIHR-ingks) to produce sounds. This vibrating **organ** is located in their throats.

Problem Solvers

Communicating and using language is just one way that parrots show they are intelligent. The story of Chango proves that these clever animals are also able to solve problems.

▲ **Chango, a double yellow-headed parrot like this one, used his beak to escape from his cage.**

One time, the owners of some parrots in Kansas went out of town. They locked all the birds in their cages. One parrot, Chango, unscrewed several bolts on the cage with his beak. The sides of the cage fell down. Chango was free! Then, Chango went to the other cages. He opened those doors, too. Many of the parrots climbed out. They were walking around when a neighbor came by to check on them.

All parrots have hooked beaks that continue to grow throughout their lives. The birds chew on hard things, like bones and wood, to keep their beaks sharp.

Tricky Birds

The person who found Chango and the other escaped parrots was surprised. The parrots probably enjoyed seeing her amazed **reaction**. Many parrots carefully watch their owners to learn how they **behave** in different situations. They use this information in many ways.

▲ Parrots, like the cockatiel, are able to mimic many of the sounds that they hear. They can even learn to whistle songs.

For example, a parrot may watch an owner move quickly to answer a phone. The bird sees that the owner is excited. So the parrot learns to make a ringing sound. The owner runs to answer the phone, but no one is there. The bird repeats the sound many times. Finally, the owner discovers the parrot is playing a trick.

▲ **Pet cockatoo**

Many parrots can learn to make the sounds of different machines, including ringing telephones and doorbells, washing machines, and beeping microwave ovens.

Caring Pets

Many owners believe their parrots understand human **emotions**. They think their pets know how they feel. People say these birds have emotional intelligence.

Parrots like to be scratched by their owners because birds in the wild do this for one another.

One woman found out that she was very ill. She went home after hearing the bad news. When her pet parrot saw her, the bird asked if she was okay. The woman was amazed. She had always asked how the bird was, but the bird had never asked that question before. Some people say that the bird was caring for his owner.

▲ **Some parrot owners think their birds understand how they feel.**

On the Wild Side

Much of the information about parrots comes from pet owners and scientists. They observe parrots in **captivity**. Some scientists wondered, however, if parrots in the wild could communicate, solve problems, and show emotions just like captive parrots.

Parrots in the Wild

Blue and gold macaw ▲

Wild parrots live in **flocks** for safety. Hawks and other animals could easily kill a bird that is alone.

North America

Atlantic Ocean

Pacific Ocean

South America

N
W   E
S

▲ **This map shows where some parrots live.**

The scientists traveled to places where wild parrots live. They watched huge flocks of parrots. They found out that these birds communicate with one another to stay safe. While the wild parrots do not use words like they do in captivity, scientists found that they communicate in different ways. They also found other signs of intelligent behavior.

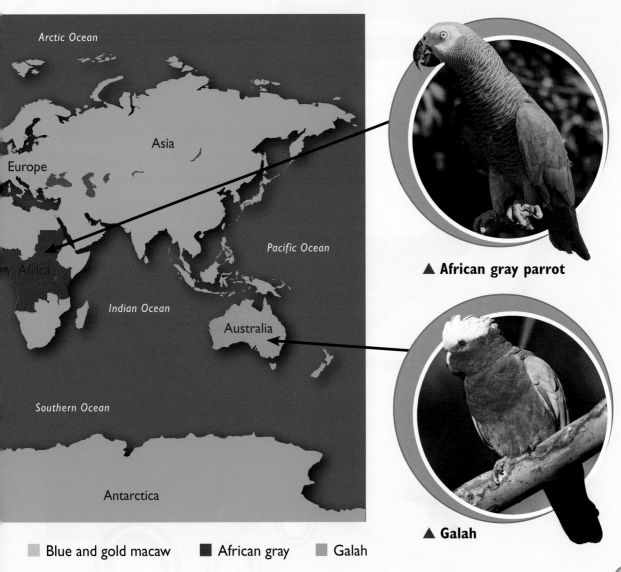

Arctic Ocean

Asia

Europe

Africa

Pacific Ocean

Indian Ocean

Australia

Southern Ocean

Antarctica

▲ African gray parrot

▲ Galah

◼ Blue and gold macaw   ◼ African gray   ◼ Galah

Guarding the Flock

When scientists watched large flocks of wild parrots feed, they noticed that some birds did not eat. They perched on branches and acted like **guards**. They were looking for **predators**. When the guard birds spotted a dangerous animal, they squawked loudly. Then the whole flock flew away.

Scientist found that some parrots looked for danger while the other parrots in the flock ate.

▲ **Hyacinth macaws are a kind of parrot that live in South America. As many as 50 of these parrots may feed together at one time.**

Guarding behavior shows that wild parrots are smart in several ways. First, the birds are working together to solve a problem. Second, the guard birds are able to remember which kinds of animals are dangerous. Third, the guards know when to sound the alarm. Finally, the birds clearly know how to communicate a message.

▲ **These hyacinth macaws take off after being frightened by a dangerous bird.**

Family Calls

Scientists found another way that wild parrots use sounds. Most parrots choose one **mate** for life. The parrot partners use sounds to communicate with each other to stay safe.

▲ **A pair of scarlet macaws**

Most parrots can produce 15 to 20 different kinds of calls. The sounds vary from loud to soft depending on the parrots' activities.

Each mate has a special chirp, or **contact call**. If parrots are separated, they call to each other to find out where their mate is. They also use calls to tell family members when they spot food or see danger.

When parrots have babies, the **chicks** learn the calls of their parents. As the babies grow, they develop their own contact calls.

▲ **A pair of galahs and their chick**

Body Language

Parrots use contact calls to communicate with their mates. They also use their bodies to communicate their feelings to other birds in the flock. To show anger, a bird will open her beak and flap her wings. A happy bird will fluff up his feathers and tuck one foot under his body. When a parrot makes his body long and thin, it means the bird is scared.

Parrots don't often bite one another. To scare away another bird, they screech loudly and flap their wings. Sometimes they lock beaks.

No matter how parrots are feeling, though, these brainy birds are fun to watch. They also make great pets. Not only can they play with you, and learn from you, but some can even talk to you.

Just the Facts

	African Gray	**Blue and Gold Macaw**
Size (from top of head to end of tail)	13 inches (33 cm)	36 inches (91 cm)
Weight	.9 pounds (408 g)	2.5 pounds (1,134 g)
Food	seeds, fruit, pollen, nectar, and sometimes insects	nuts, seeds, fruit
Life Span	50 or more years	about 80 years
Habitat	rain forests in Africa	forests and swamps in South America

More Smart Parrots

Jimbo is an African gray parrot that lives in Arkansas. One day Jimbo was looking out the window and saw a roadrunner. Jimbo said to her owner, "Momma, look! A bird!"

Spectacled parrotlets are a kind of parrot that give "names" to one another. They make a call that is used to get the attention of one individual parrot. When scientists recorded the calls and played them back to a group of spectacled parrotlets, only the birds whose "names" were called turned their heads to look around.

◄ **Spectacled parrotlet**

Glossary

beaks (BEEKS) the hard, horn-shaped part of a bird's mouth

behave (bi-HAYV) act

captivity (kap-TIV-uh-tee) places where animals live in which they are cared for by people, and which are not the animals' natural environments

chicks (CHIKS) baby birds

communicate (kuh-MYOO-ni-kayt) to share information, ideas, feelings, and thoughts

contact call (KON-takt CAWL) a special sound made by a parrot

emotions (i-MOH-shuhnz) feelings

flocks (FLOKS) a group of the same kind of animal that lives together

guards (GARDZ) people or animals who watch over or protect a place or person

intelligent (in-TEL-uh-juhnt) smart

language (LANG-gwij) the words that people speak or write

mate (MATE) a male or female partner

materials (muh-TIHR-ee-uhlz) what things are made of

mimic (MIM-ik) copy

organ (OR-guhn) a body part that does a particular job

predators (PRED-uh-turz) animals that hunt other animals for food

reaction (ree-AK-shuhn) a response to something that happened

Bibliography

Linden, Eugene. *The Parrot's Lament: And Other True Tales of Animal Intrigue, Intelligence, and Ingenuity.* New York: Plume Books (2000).

Pepperberg, Irene Maxine. *The Alex Studies: Cognitive and Communicative Abilities of Grey Parrots.* Cambridge, Massachusetts: Harvard University Press (2000).

Sparks, John. *Parrots: A Natural History.* New York: Checkmark Books (1990).

www.birdsnways.com/wisdom/ww43eiv.htm

www.sheldrake.org/nkisi

Read More

Flanagan, Alice. *Talking Birds.* Danbury, CT: Children's Press (1996).

Gerholdt, James E. *Amazon Parrots.* Edina, MN: Abdo & Daughters Publishing (1997).

Rauzon, Mark J. *Parrots Around the World.* New York: Franklin Watts (2001).

Learn More Online

Visit these Web sites to learn more about parrots:

http://news.nationalgeographic.com/kids/2004/03/parrot.html

www.nationalparks.nsw.gov.au/npws.nsf/Content/Parrots

Index

About the Author

Margaret Fetty has been a writer and editor of
educational materials for over 15 years. She has written
13 books for young readers.